This book belongs to

....

Message from Sophia

When I was told me that colouring in, doing grounding and mindfulness activities would help me feel better I knew it was wrong. And I was right. It didn't initially help me feel better. But it did eventually help me to find better ways to cope with my emotions.

Message from Nessie Mac

Sometimes our minds say horrible and negative things to us. And I know that we sometimes listen. But I don't want you to. I want you to think of yourself as fearless, smart, important. And so much more. Yes, life is tough but so are you.

What is Mindfulness Colouring?

Sometimes we can get upset, angry or our emotions are just all over the place, thinking of the past and sometimes the future. Mindfulness colouring allows you to think of the here and now. You may start off with your mind everywhere but as you colour in your breath slows down and you can focus, you can think, you can breathe.

What is grounding?

When your negative emotions are getting the better of you by doing the 5-4-3-2-1 grounding technique it will help your brain to calm down and because you are able to recognize where are and you will be comforted. This in turn will help you to feel more in control of the situation.

Take good care of yourself, for yourself!

I AM
FREE TO
BE ME

This is called the 5-4-3-2-1 Grounding Technique.
It should help you to focus.

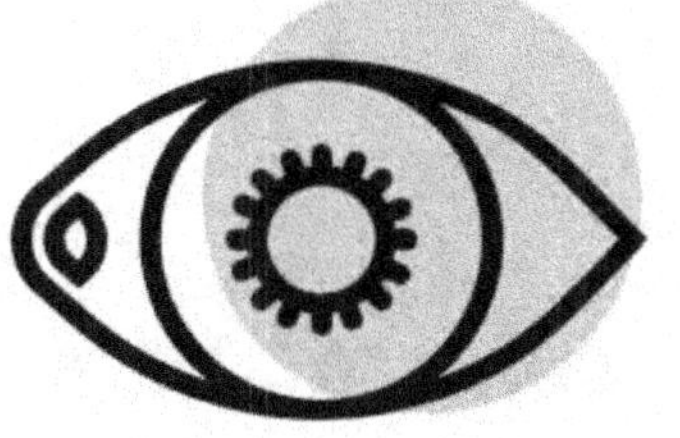

Step 1 – Name FIVE things you can see

Step 2 – Name FOUR things you can touch

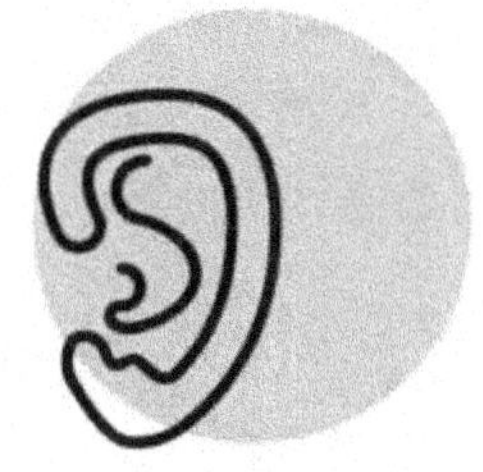

Step 3 – Name THREE things you can hear

Step 4 – Name TWO things you can smell

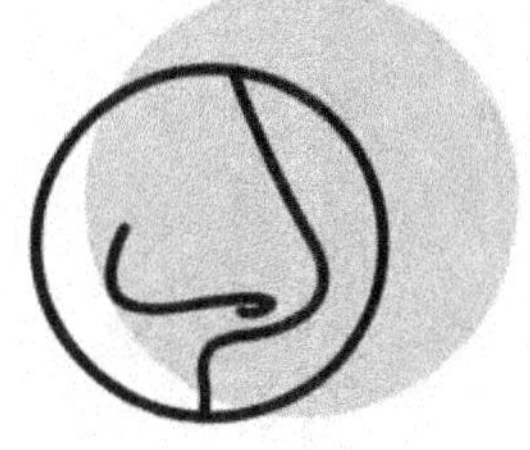

Step 5 – Name ONE thing you like the taste of

You've got this!

Circle of Control

Things I CANNOT control
I will let go of these

Things I CAN Control
I will focus on these

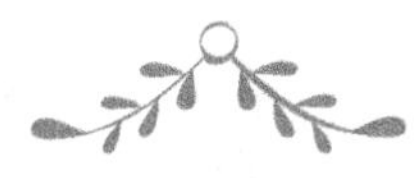

Happy Memory Clouds

Fill out these clouds as you think of happy memories.
Use them when your emotions become too much.

What were you doing?

Where were you?

Who was there?

What could you hear?

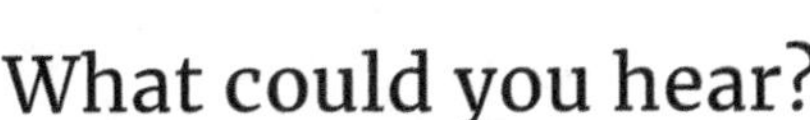

What could you smell?

Grounding Yourself

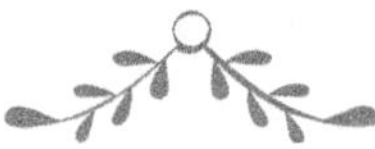

What is your name?.......................................

Where are you

Words that describe your space

Who is with you? What are they doing?

Words that describe your feelings

What do you hear?

What do you see?

What can you smell?

What can you touch?

When you are calm, set an intention.

Body Scan

Today's date........................... Time....................

Where are you?..

Head and Face

Neck and Shoulders

Back

Chest

Stomach

Arms

Legs

Whole body sensations

Sensations

warm – cold – soft – hard – breeze – damp – dry
tense – strong – taut – numb – tingling – tickling – muscle
slender – fragile - pressure – throbbing – blocked – pulse
stabbing – quivering - nauseous – shaking – aching – breathless
wired – anxious - soothed – relaxed – comfortable

Finger Labyrinth

Use your finger to slowly trace a path to the center of the labyrinth

Breathe calmly and slowly as you focus.
When you reach the center, draw a long deep breath or two.

Then trace your path back to the outside
Repeat until you feel more focused and calm.

Focus Words

Breathe - Peace - Relax - Tranquility - Serenity - Calm - Space - Beauty
Love - Wonder - Kindness - Light - Happiness - Joy - Warmth

I AM
INTELLIGENT

This is called the 5-4-3-2-1 Grounding Technique.
It should help you to focus.

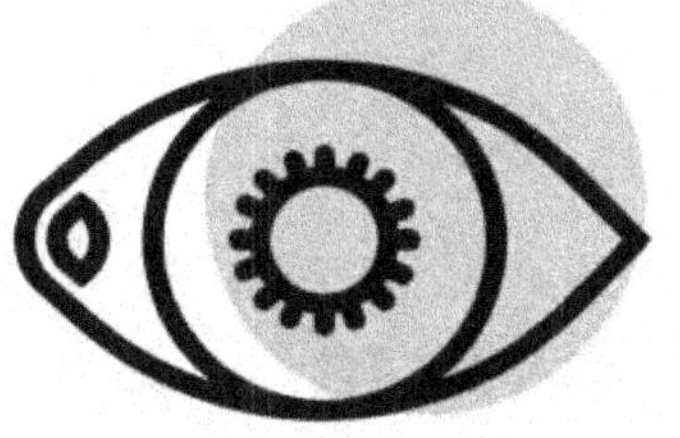

Step 1 – Name FIVE things you can see

Step 2 – Name FOUR things you can touch

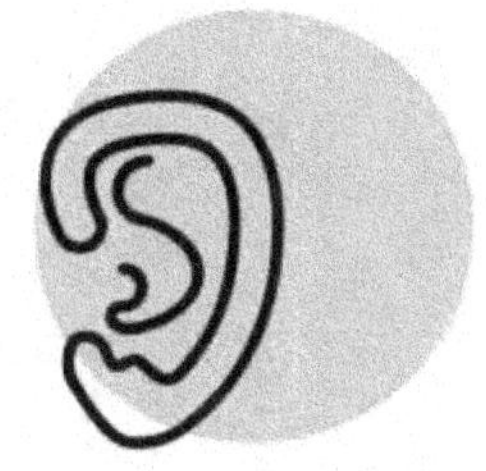

Step 3 – Name THREE things you can hear

Step 4 – Name TWO things you can smell

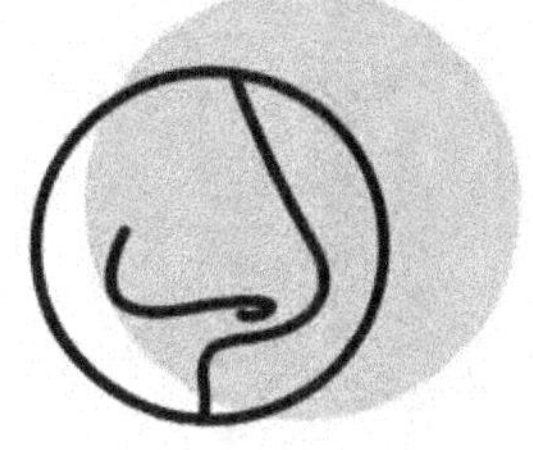

Step 5 – Name ONE thing you like the taste of

You've got this!

Circle of Control

Things I CANNOT control
I will let go of these

Things I CAN Control
I will focus on these

Happy Memory Clouds

Fill out these clouds as you think of happy memories.
Use them when your emotions become too much.

What were you doing?

Where were you?

Who was there?

What could you smell?

What could you hear?

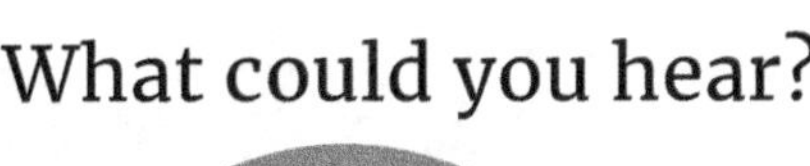

Grounding Yourself

What is your name?................................

Where are you

Words that describe your space

Who is with you? What are they doing?

Words that describe your feelings

What do you hear?

What do you see?

What can you smell?

What can you touch?

When you are calm, set an intention.

Body Scan

Today's date............................   Time....................

Where are you?...

Head and Face

Neck and Shoulders

Back

Legs

Chest

Stomach

Arms

Whole body sensations

Sensations

warm – cold – soft – hard – breeze – damp – dry
tense – strong – taut – numb – tingling – tickling – muscle
slender – fragile - pressure – throbbing – blocked – pulse
stabbing – quivering - nauseous – shaking – aching – breathless
wired – anxious - soothed – relaxed – comfortable

Finger Labyrinth

Use your finger to slowly trace a path to the center of the labyrinth

Breathe calmly and slowly as you focus.
When you reach the center, draw a long deep breath or two.

Then trace your path back to the outside
Repeat until you feel more focused and calm.

Focus Words

Breathe - Peace - Relax - Tranquility - Serenity - Calm - Space - Beauty
Love - Wonder - Kindness - Light - Happiness - Joy - Warmth

I AM HERE
FOR A
REASON

This is called the 5-4-3-2-1 Grounding Technique.
It should help you to focus.

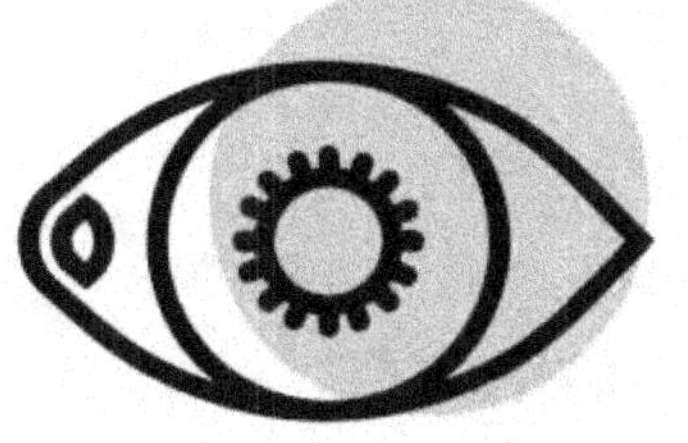

Step 1 – Name FIVE things you can see

Step 2 – Name FOUR things you can touch

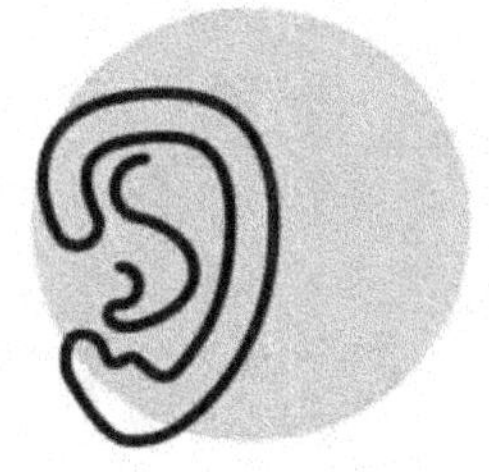

Step 3 – Name THREE things you can hear

Step 4 – Name TWO things you can smell

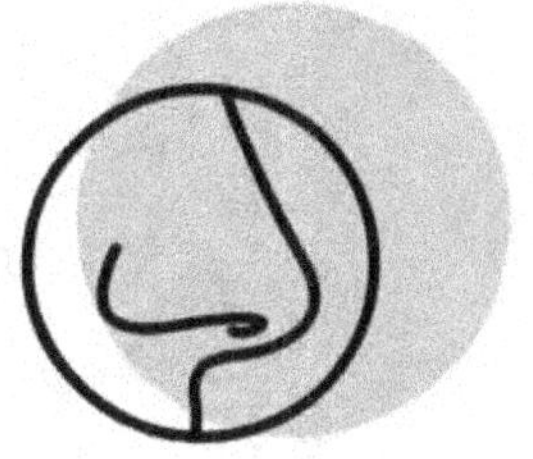

Step 5 – Name ONE thing you like the taste of

You've got this!

Circle of Control

Things I CANNOT control
I will let go of these

Things I CAN Control
I will focus on these

Happy Memory Clouds

Fill out these clouds as you think of happy memories.
Use them when your emotions become too much.

What were you doing?

Where were you?

Who was there?

What could you hear?

What could you smell?

Grounding Yourself

What is your name?......................................

Where are you

Words that describe your space

Who is with you? What are they doing?

Words that describe your feelings

What do you hear?

What do you see?

What can you smell?

What can you touch?

When you are calm, set an intention.

Body Scan

Today's date............................   Time....................

Where are you?...

Head and Face

Neck and Shoulders

Back

Legs

Chest

Stomach

Arms

Whole body sensations

Sensations

warm – cold – soft – hard – breeze – damp – dry
tense – strong – taut – numb – tingling – tickling – muscle
slender – fragile - pressure – throbbing – blocked – pulse
stabbing – quivering - nauseous – shaking – aching – breathless
wired – anxious - soothed – relaxed – comfortable

Finger Labyrinth

Use your finger to slowly trace a path to the center of the labyrinth

Breathe calmly and slowly as you focus.
When you reach the center, draw a long deep breath or two.

Then trace your path back to the outside
Repeat until you feel more focused and calm.

Focus Words

Breathe - Peace - Relax - Tranquility - Serenity - Calm - Space - Beauty
Love - Wonder - Kindness - Light - Happiness - Joy - Warmth

TODAY
IS A
NEW DAY

This is called the 5-4-3-2-1 Grounding Technique.
It should help you to focus.

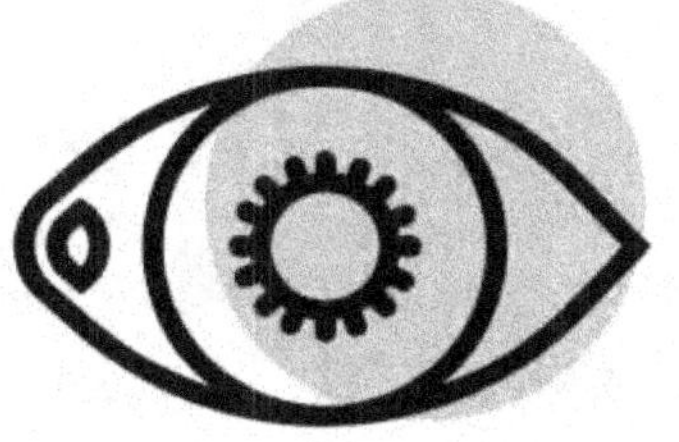

Step 1 – Name FIVE things you can see

Step 2 – Name FOUR things you can touch

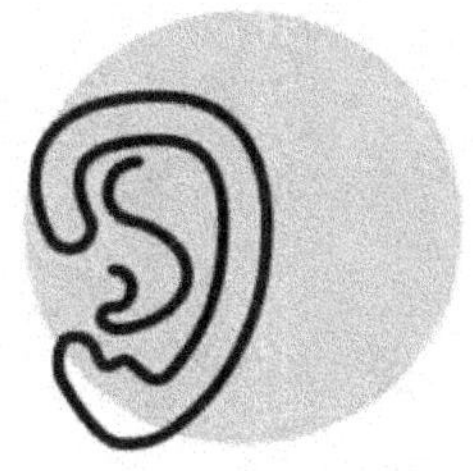

Step 3 – Name THREE things you can hear

Step 4 – Name TWO things you can smell

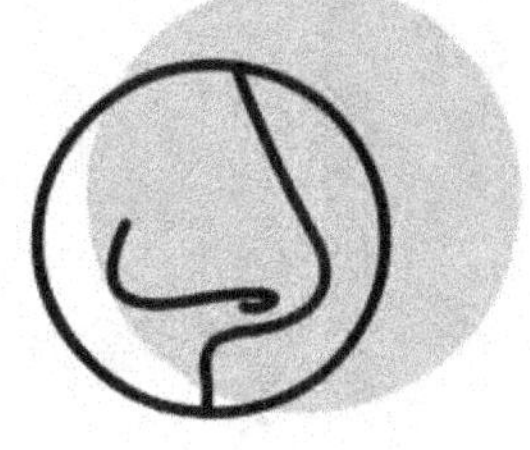

Step 5 – Name ONE thing you like the taste of

You've got this!

Circle of Control

Things I CANNOT control
I will let go of these

Things I CAN Control
I will focus on these

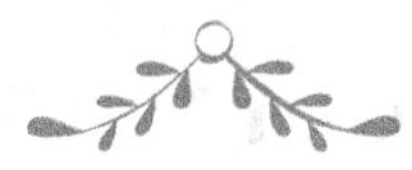

Happy Memory Clouds

Fill out these clouds as you think of happy memories.
Use them when your emotions become too much.

What were you doing?

Where were you?

Who was there?

What could you hear?

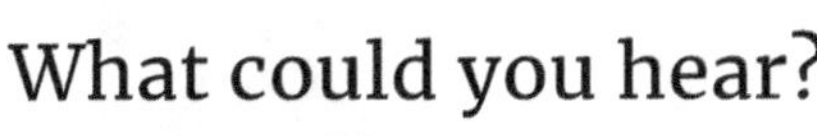

What could you smell?

Grounding Yourself

What is your name?.....................................

Where are you

Words that describe your space

Who is with you? What are they doing?

Words that describe your feelings

What do you hear?

What do you see?

What can you smell?

What can you touch?

When you are calm, set an intention.

Body Scan

Today's date...........................   Time...................

Where are you?...

Head and Face

Neck and Shoulders

Back

Legs

Chest

Stomach

Arms

Whole body sensations

Sensations

warm – cold – soft – hard – breeze – damp – dry
tense – strong – taut – numb – tingling – tickling – muscle
slender – fragile - pressure – throbbing – blocked – pulse
stabbing – quivering - nauseous – shaking – aching – breathless
wired – anxious - soothed – relaxed – comfortable

Finger Labyrinth

Use your finger to slowly trace a path to the center of the labyrinth

Breathe calmly and slowly as you focus.
When you reach the center, draw a long deep breath or two.

Then trace your path back to the outside
Repeat until you feel more focused and calm.

Focus Words

Breathe - Peace - Relax - Tranquility - Serenity - Calm - Space - Beauty
Love - Wonder - Kindness - Light - Happiness - Joy - Warmth

I'M
GONNA BE
THE BEST
I CAN BE

This is called the 5-4-3-2-1 Grounding Technique.
It should help you to focus.

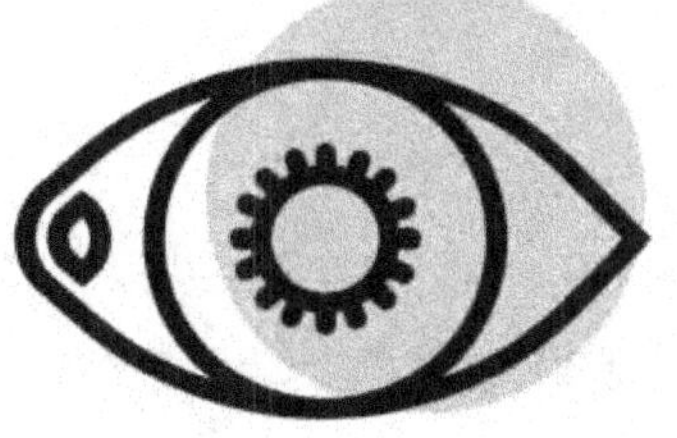

Step 1 – Name FIVE things you can see

Step 2 – Name FOUR things you can touch

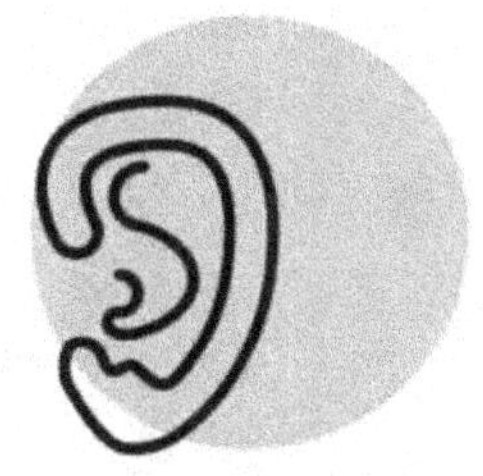

Step 3 – Name THREE things you can hear

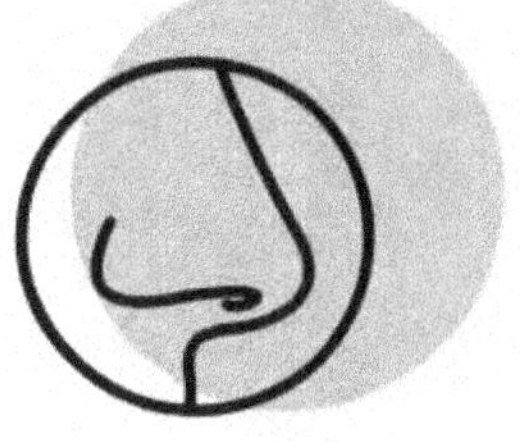

Step 4 – Name TWO things you can smell

Step 5 – Name ONE thing you like the taste of

You've got this!

Circle of Control

Things I CANNOT control
I will let go of these

Things I CAN Control
I will focus on these

Happy Memory Clouds

Fill out these clouds as you think of happy memories.
Use them when your emotions become too much.

What were you doing?

Where were you?

Who was there?

What could you hear?

What could you smell?

Grounding Yourself

What is your name?......................................

Where are you

Words that describe your space

Who is with you? What are they doing?

Words that describe your feelings

What do you hear?

What do you see?

What can you smell?

What can you touch?

When you are calm, set an intention.

Body Scan

Today's date.......................... Time....................

Where are you?..

Head and Face

Neck and Shoulders

Back

Legs

Chest

Stomach

Arms

Whole body sensations

Sensations

warm – cold – soft – hard – breeze – damp – dry
tense – strong – taut – numb – tingling – tickling – muscle
slender – fragile - pressure – throbbing – blocked – pulse
stabbing – quivering - nauseous – shaking – aching – breathless
wired – anxious - soothed – relaxed – comfortable

Finger Labyrinth

Use your finger to slowly trace a path to the center of the labyrinth

Breathe calmly and slowly as you focus.
When you reach the center, draw a long deep breath or two.

Then trace your path back to the outside
Repeat until you feel more focused and calm.

Focus Words

Breathe - Peace - Relax - Tranquility - Serenity - Calm - Space - Beauty
Love - Wonder - Kindness - Light - Happiness - Joy - Warmth

I CAN DO
ANYTHING
BUT NOT
EVERYTHING

This is called the 5-4-3-2-1 Grounding Technique.
It should help you to focus.

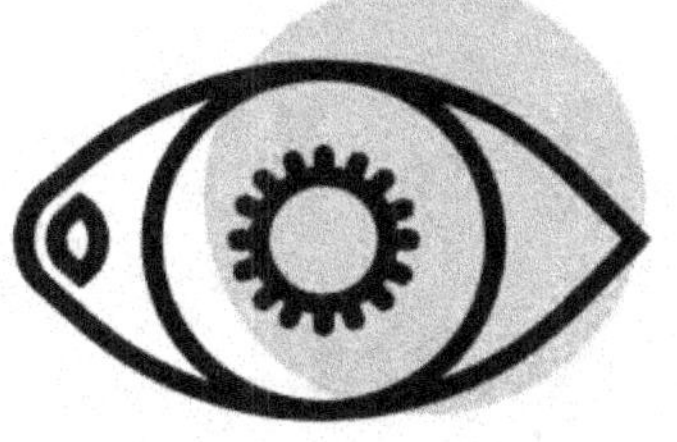

Step 1 – Name FIVE things you can see

Step 2 – Name FOUR things you can touch

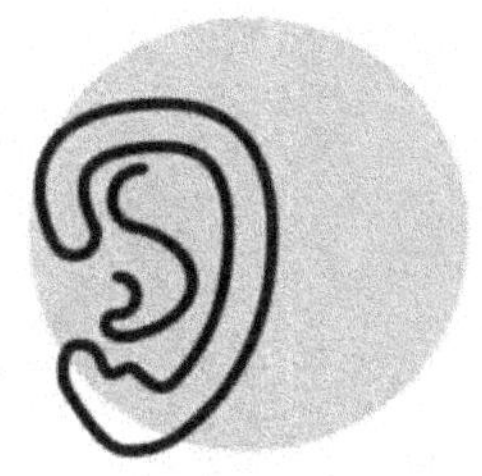

Step 3 – Name THREE things you can hear

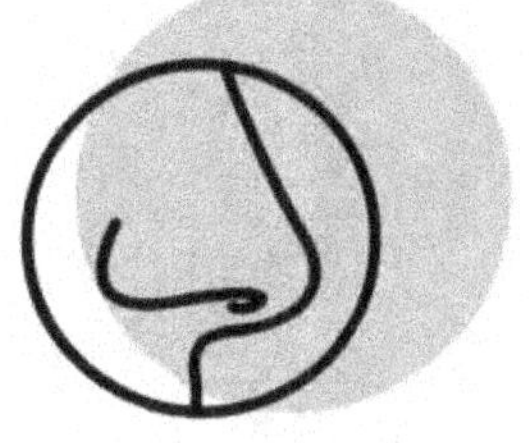

Step 4 – Name TWO things you can smell

Step 5 – Name ONE thing you like the taste of

You've got this!

Circle of Control

Things I CANNOT control
I will let go of these

Things I CAN Control
I will focus on these

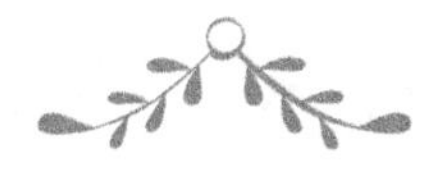

Happy Memory Clouds

Fill out these clouds as you think of happy memories.
Use them when your emotions become too much.

What were you doing?

Where were you?

Who was there?

What could you hear?

What could you smell?

Grounding Yourself

What is your name?....................................

Where are you

Words that describe your space

Who is with you? What are they doing?

Words that describe your feelings

What do you hear?

What do you see?

What can you smell?

What can you touch?

When you are calm, set an intention.

Body Scan

Today's date............................. Time...................

Where are you?..

Head and Face

Neck and Shoulders

Back

Legs

Chest

Stomach

Arms

Whole body sensations

Sensations

warm – cold – soft – hard – breeze – damp – dry
tense – strong – taut – numb – tingling – tickling – muscle
slender – fragile - pressure – throbbing – blocked – pulse
stabbing – quivering - nauseous – shaking – aching – breathless
wired – anxious - soothed – relaxed – comfortable

Finger Labyrinth

Use your finger to slowly trace a path to the center of the labyrinth

Breathe calmly and slowly as you focus.
When you reach the center, draw a long deep breath or two.

Then trace your path back to the outside
Repeat until you feel more focused and calm.

Focus Words

Breathe - Peace - Relax - Tranquility - Serenity - Calm - Space - Beauty
Love - Wonder - Kindness - Light - Happiness - Joy - Warmth

I AM
WHO
I AM

This is called the 5-4-3-2-1 Grounding Technique.
It should help you to focus.

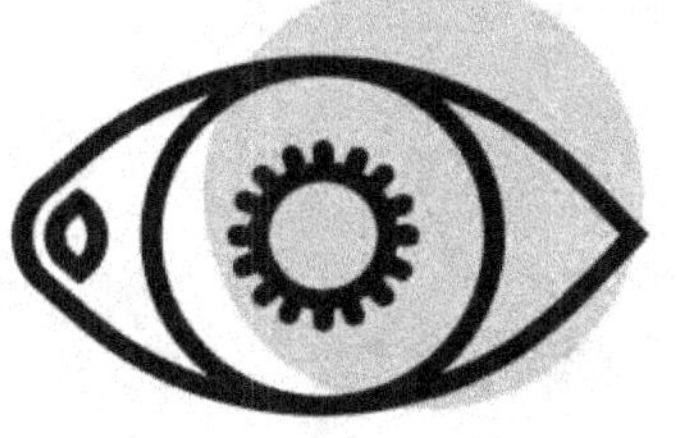

Step 1 – Name FIVE things you can see

Step 2 – Name FOUR things you can touch

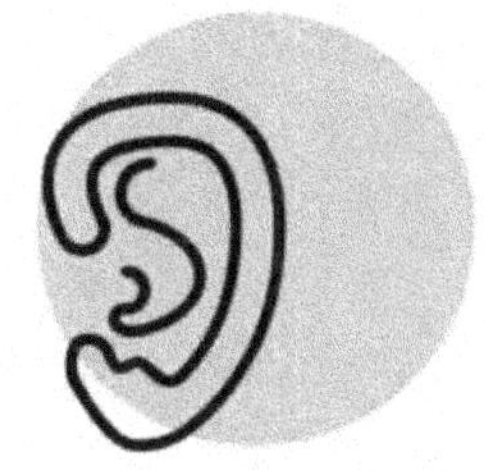

Step 3 – Name THREE things you can hear

Step 4 – Name TWO things you can smell

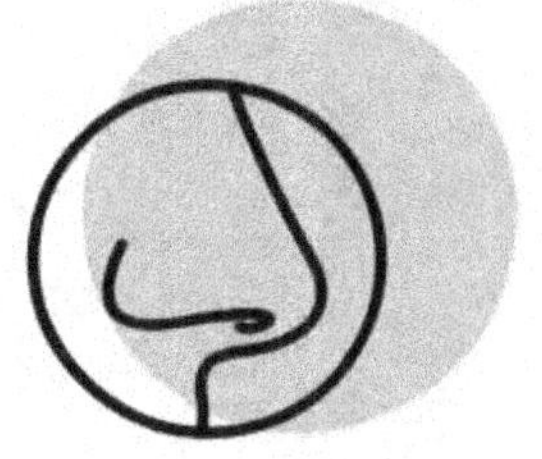

Step 5 – Name ONE thing you like the taste of

You've got this!

Circle of Control

Things I CANNOT control
I will let go of these

Things I CAN Control
I will focus on these

Happy Memory Clouds

Fill out these clouds as you think of happy memories.
Use them when your emotions become too much.

What were you doing?

Where were you?

Who was there?

What could you hear?

What could you smell?

Grounding Yourself

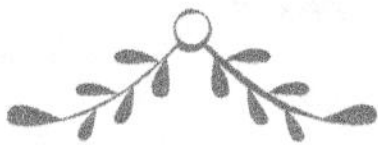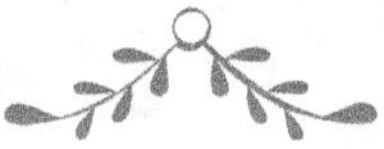

What is your name?.....................................

Where are you

Words that describe your space

Who is with you? What are they doing?

Words that describe your feelings

What do you hear?

What do you see?

What can you smell?

What can you touch?

When you are calm, set an intention.

Body Scan

Today's date...........................   Time....................

Where are you?..

Head and Face

Neck and Shoulders

Back

Legs

Chest

Stomach

Arms

Whole body sensations

Sensations

warm – cold – soft – hard – breeze – damp – dry
tense – strong – taut – numb – tingling – tickling – muscle
slender – fragile - pressure – throbbing – blocked – pulse
stabbing – quivering - nauseous – shaking – aching – breathless
wired – anxious - soothed – relaxed – comfortable

Finger Labyrinth

Use your finger to slowly trace a path to the center of the labyrinth

Breathe calmly and slowly as you focus.
When you reach the center, draw a long deep breath or two.

Then trace your path back to the outside
Repeat until you feel more focused and calm.

Focus Words

Breathe - Peace - Relax - Tranquility - Serenity - Calm - Space - Beauty
Love - Wonder - Kindness - Light - Happiness - Joy - Warmth

I CONTROL
MY MIND

This is called the 5-4-3-2-1 Grounding Technique. It should help you to focus.

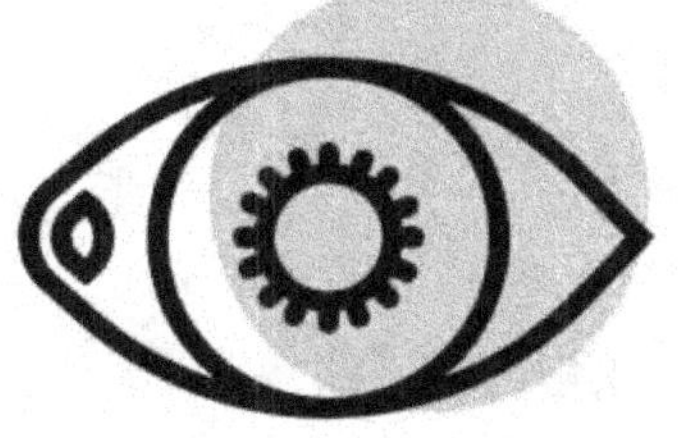

Step 1 – Name FIVE things you can see

Step 2 – Name FOUR things you can touch

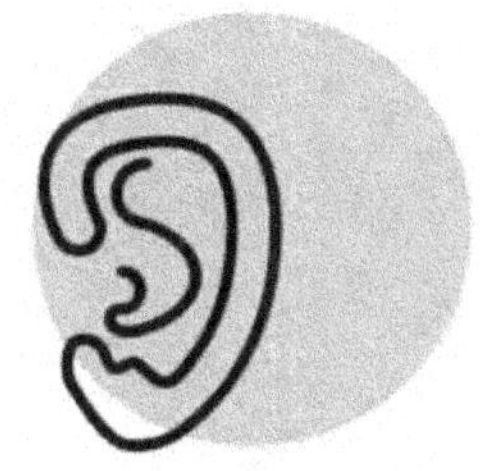

Step 3 – Name THREE things you can hear

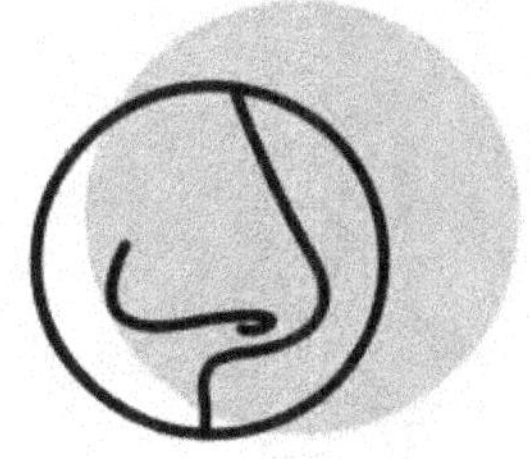

Step 4 – Name TWO things you can smell

Step 5 – Name ONE thing you like the taste of

You've got this!

Circle of Control

Things I CANNOT control
I will let go of these

Things I CAN Control
I will focus on these

Happy Memory Clouds

Fill out these clouds as you think of happy memories.
Use them when your emotions become too much.

What were you doing?

Where were you?

Who was there?

What could you smell?

What could you hear?

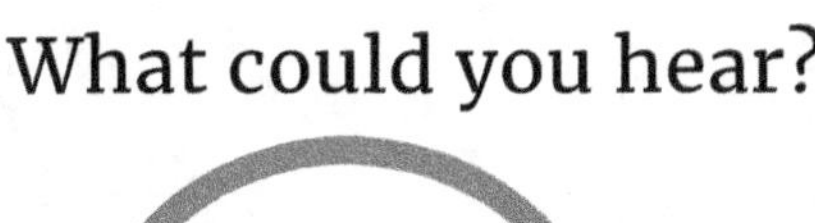

Grounding Yourself

What is your name?.....................................

Where are you

Words that describe your space

Who is with you? What are they doing?

Words that describe your feelings

What do you hear?

What do you see?

What can you smell?

What can you touch?

When you are calm, set an intention.

Body Scan

Today's date..........................   Time....................

Where are you?..

Head and Face

Neck and Shoulders

Back

Legs

Chest

Stomach

Arms

Whole body sensations

Sensations

warm – cold – soft – hard – breeze – damp – dry
tense – strong – taut – numb – tingling – tickling – muscle
slender – fragile - pressure – throbbing – blocked – pulse
stabbing – quivering - nauseous – shaking – aching – breathless
wired – anxious - soothed – relaxed – comfortable

Finger Labyrinth

Use your finger to slowly trace a path to the center of the labyrinth

Breathe calmly and slowly as you focus.
When you reach the center, draw a long deep breath or two.

Then trace your path back to the outside
Repeat until you feel more focused and calm.

Focus Words

Breathe - Peace - Relax - Tranquility - Serenity - Calm - Space - Beauty
Love - Wonder - Kindness - Light - Happiness - Joy - Warmth

I WILL NOT
COMPARE
MYSELF
TO OTHERS

This is called the 5-4-3-2-1 Grounding Technique. It should help you to focus.

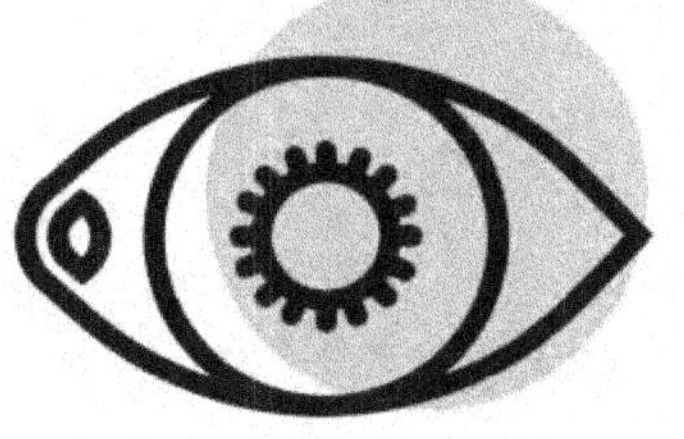

Step 1 – Name FIVE things you can see

Step 2 – Name FOUR things you can touch

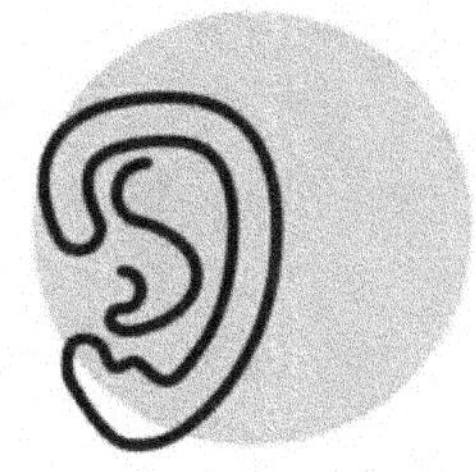

Step 3 – Name THREE things you can hear

Step 4 – Name TWO things you can smell

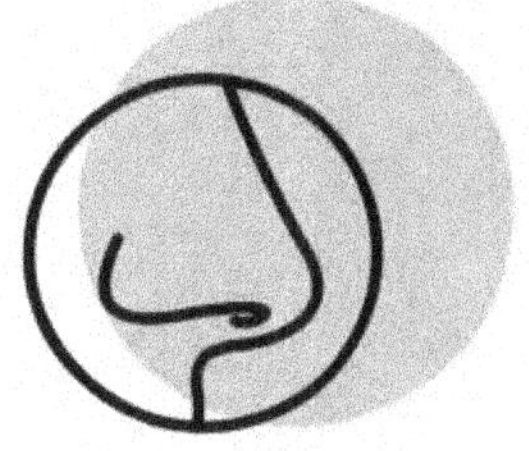

Step 5 – Name ONE thing you like the taste of

You've got this!

Circle of Control

Things I CANNOT control
I will let go of these

Things I CAN Control
I will focus on these

Happy Memory Clouds

Fill out these clouds as you think of happy memories.
Use them when your emotions become too much.

What were you doing?

Where were you?

Who was there?

What could you hear?

What could you smell?

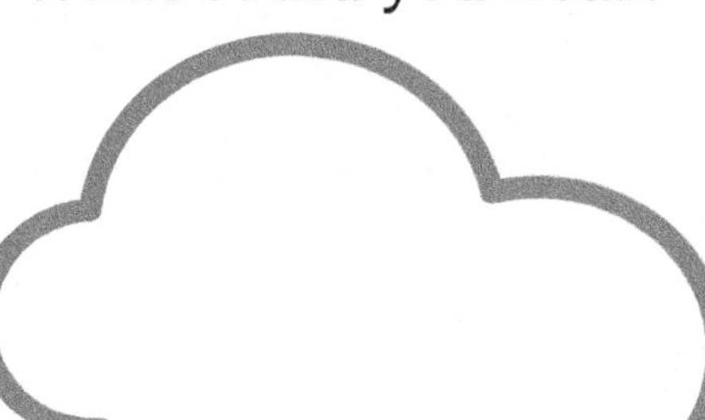

Grounding Yourself

What is your name?......................................

Where are you

Words that describe your space

Who is with you? What are they doing?

Words that describe your feelings

What do you hear?

What do you see?

What can you smell?

What can you touch?

When you are calm, set an intention.

Body Scan

Today's date............................   Time....................

Where are you?..

Head and Face

Neck and Shoulders

Back

Chest

Stomach

Arms

Legs

Whole body sensations

Sensations

warm – cold – soft – hard – breeze – damp – dry
tense – strong – taut – numb – tingling – tickling – muscle
slender – fragile - pressure – throbbing – blocked – pulse
stabbing – quivering - nauseous – shaking – aching – breathless
wired – anxious - soothed – relaxed – comfortable

Finger Labyrinth

Use your finger to slowly trace a path to the center of the labyrinth

Breathe calmly and slowly as you focus.
When you reach the center, draw a long deep breath or two.

Then trace your path back to the outside
Repeat until you feel more focused and calm.

Focus Words

Breathe - Peace - Relax - Tranquility - Serenity - Calm - Space - Beauty
Love - Wonder - Kindness - Light - Happiness - Joy - Warmth

I'VE
GOT THIS

This is called the 5-4-3-2-1 Grounding Technique.
It should help you to focus.

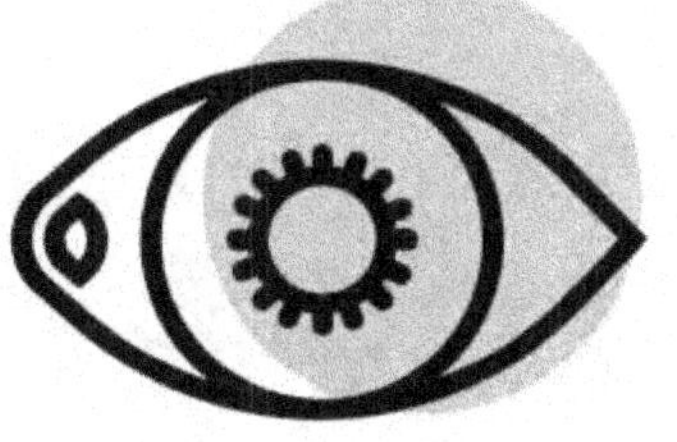

Step 1 – Name FIVE things you can see

Step 2 – Name FOUR things you can touch

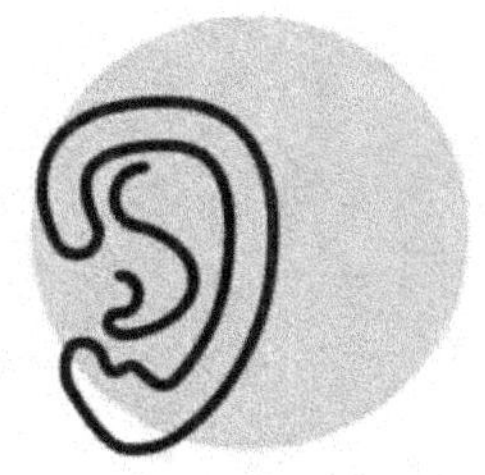

Step 3 – Name THREE things you can hear

Step 4 – Name TWO things you can smell

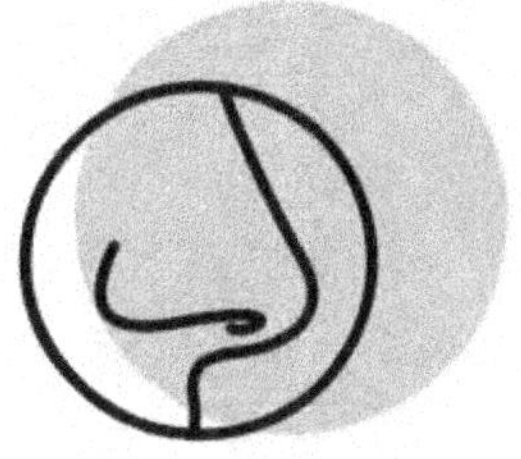

Step 5 – Name ONE thing you like the taste of

You've got this!

Circle of Control

Things I CANNOT control
I will let go of these

Things I CAN Control
I will focus on these

Happy Memory Clouds

Fill out these clouds as you think of happy memories.
Use them when your emotions become too much.

What were you doing?

Where were you?

Who was there?

What could you hear?

What could you smell?

Grounding Yourself

What is your name?......................................

Where are you

Words that describe your space

Who is with you? What are they doing?

Words that describe your feelings

What do you hear?

What do you see?

What can you smell?

What can you touch?

When you are calm, set an intention.

Body Scan

Today's date...........................   Time...................

Where are you?...

Head and Face

Neck and Shoulders

Back

Legs

Chest

Stomach

Arms

Whole body sensations

Sensations

warm – cold – soft – hard – breeze – damp – dry
tense – strong – taut – numb – tingling – tickling – muscle
slender – fragile - pressure – throbbing – blocked – pulse
stabbing – quivering - nauseous – shaking – aching – breathless
wired – anxious - soothed – relaxed – comfortable

Finger Labyrinth

Use your finger to slowly trace a path to the center of the labyrinth

Breathe calmly and slowly as you focus.
When you reach the center, draw a long deep breath or two.

Then trace your path back to the outside
Repeat until you feel more focused and calm.

Focus Words

Breathe - Peace - Relax - Tranquility - Serenity - Calm - Space - Beauty
Love - Wonder - Kindness - Light - Happiness - Joy - Warmth

I MATTER

This is called the 5-4-3-2-1 Grounding Technique. It should help you to focus.

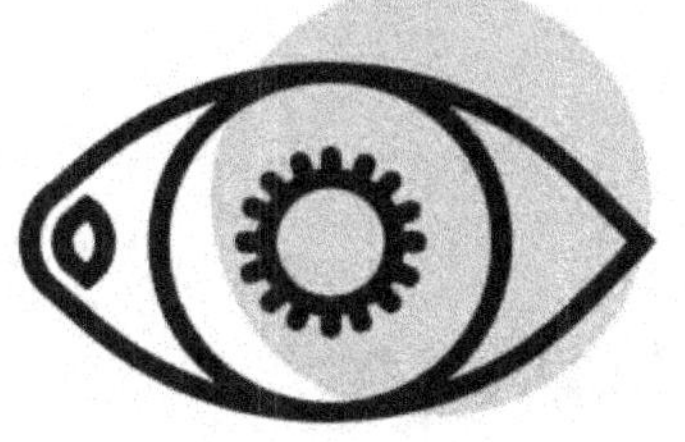

Step 1 – Name FIVE things you can see

Step 2 – Name FOUR things you can touch

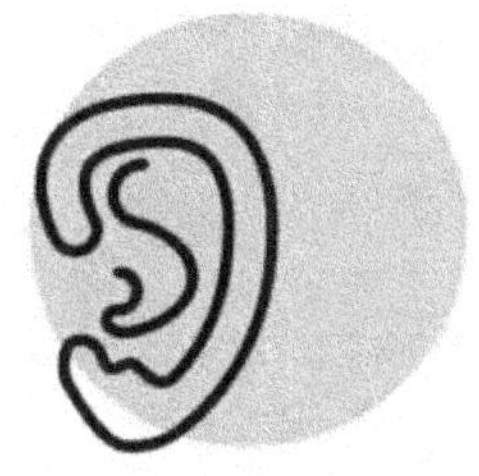

Step 3 – Name THREE things you can hear

Step 4 – Name TWO things you can smell

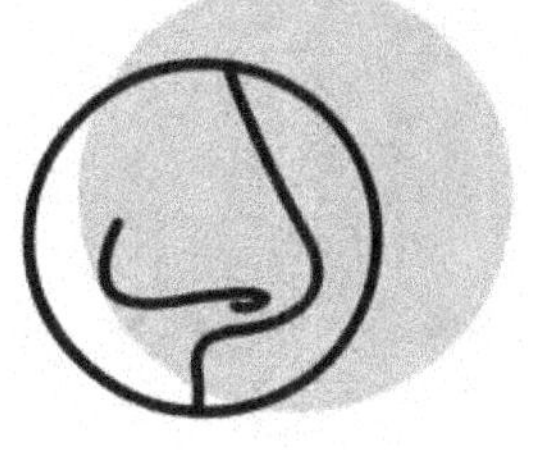

Step 5 – Name ONE thing you like the taste of

You've got this!

Circle of Control

Things I CANNOT control
I will let go of these

Things I CAN Control
I will focus on these

Happy Memory Clouds

Fill out these clouds as you think of happy memories.
Use them when your emotions become too much.

What were you doing?

Where were you?

Who was there?

What could you hear?

What could you smell?

Grounding Yourself

What is your name?..

Where are you

Words that describe your space

Who is with you? What are they doing?

Words that describe your feelings

What do you hear?

What do you see?

What can you smell?

What can you touch?

When you are calm, set an intention.

Body Scan

Today's date........................   Time...................

Where are you?..

Head and Face

Neck and Shoulders

Back

Chest

Stomach

Arms

Legs

Whole body sensations

Sensations

warm – cold – soft – hard – breeze – damp – dry
tense – strong – taut – numb – tingling – tickling – muscle
slender – fragile - pressure – throbbing – blocked – pulse
stabbing – quivering - nauseous – shaking – aching – breathless
wired – anxious - soothed – relaxed – comfortable

Finger Labyrinth

Use your finger to slowly trace a path to the center of the labyrinth

Breathe calmly and slowly as you focus.
When you reach the center, draw a long deep breath or two.

Then trace your path back to the outside
Repeat until you feel more focused and calm.

Focus Words

Breathe - Peace - Relax - Tranquility - Serenity - Calm - Space - Beauty
Love - Wonder - Kindness - Light - Happiness - Joy - Warmth

I CONTROL
MY
THOUGHTS

This is called the 5-4-3-2-1 Grounding Technique.
It should help you to focus.

Step 1 – Name FIVE things you can see

Step 2 – Name FOUR things you can touch

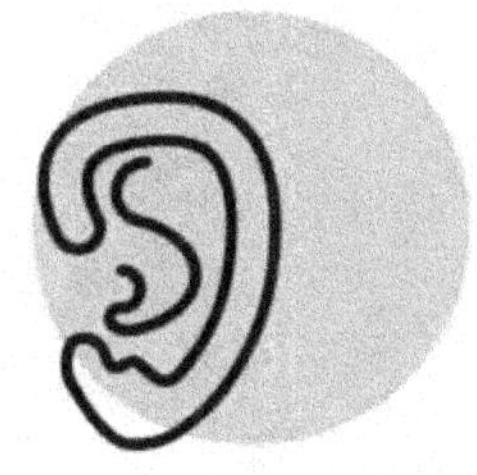

Step 3 – Name THREE things you can hear

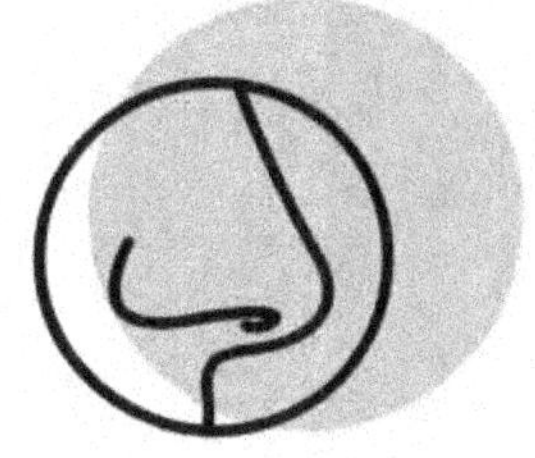

Step 4 – Name TWO things you can smell

Step 5 – Name ONE thing you like the taste of

You've got this!

Circle of Control

Things I CANNOT control
I will let go of these

Things I CAN Control
I will focus on these

Happy Memory Clouds

Fill out these clouds as you think of happy memories.
Use them when your emotions become too much.

What were you doing?

Where were you?

Who was there?

What could you hear?

What could you smell?

Grounding Yourself

What is your name?......................................

Where are you

Words that describe your space

Who is with you? What are they doing?

Words that describe your feelings

What do you hear?

What do you see?

What can you smell?

What can you touch?

When you are calm, set an intention.

Body Scan

Today's date...........................   Time....................

Where are you?...

Head and Face

Neck and Shoulders

Back

Chest

Stomach

Arms

Legs

Whole body sensations

Sensations

warm – cold – soft – hard – breeze – damp – dry
tense – strong – taut – numb – tingling – tickling – muscle
slender – fragile - pressure – throbbing – blocked – pulse
stabbing – quivering - nauseous – shaking – aching – breathless
wired – anxious - soothed – relaxed – comfortable

Finger Labyrinth

Use your finger to slowly trace a path to the center of the labyrinth

Breathe calmly and slowly as you focus.
When you reach the center, draw a long deep breath or two.

Then trace your path back to the outside
Repeat until you feel more focused and calm.

Focus Words

Breathe - Peace - Relax - Tranquility - Serenity - Calm - Space - Beauty
Love - Wonder - Kindness - Light - Happiness - Joy - Warmth

The 'Me' I Am

There are four books in the series:

* Red Book
* Blue Book
* Yellow Book
Please note that ALL the activities are the same BUT all the colouring pages are
different in each of the above THREE books
PLUS
* Indigo Book - all the colouring pages of the previous books for you to colour, cut
out and keep) plus bonus colouring pages.